FAITHFUL COLORS

A Bible Verse Coloring Book for Reflection and Relaxation

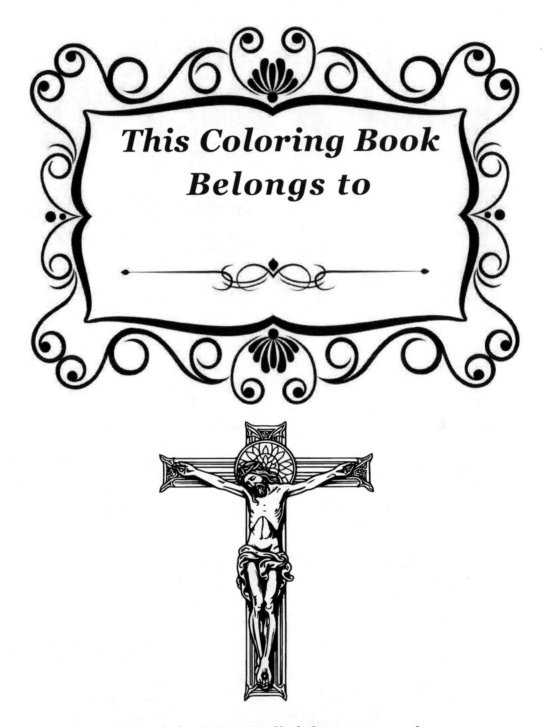

This Coloring Book Belongs to

Test Your Colours Here

God's mercy and grace are new every morning.

-Lamentations 3:22

For God so loved the world that he gave his one and only Son, that whoever believes in him shall not perish but have eternal life.

-John 3:16

For I know the plans I have for you, declares the LORD, plans to prosper you and not to harm you, plans to give you hope and a future.

—Jeremiah 29:11

And we know that in all things God works for the good of those who love him, who have been called according to his purpose.

-Romans 8:28

And the peace of God, which transcends all understanding, will guard your hearts and your minds in Christ Jesus.

-Philippians 4:7

Do not conform any longer to the pattern of this world, but be transformed by the renewing of your mind. Then you will be able to test and approve what God's will is —his good, pleasing and perfect will.

-2 Chronicles 20:15

All Scripture is God-breathed and is useful for teaching, rebuking, correcting and training in righteousness.

-2 Timothy 3:16

And without faith it is impossible to please God.

—2 Chronicles 20:15

He was crushed for our iniquities; the punishment that brought us peace was on him, and by his wounds we are healed.

-2 Chronicles 20:15

But the fruit of the Spirit is love, joy, peace, forbearance, kindness, goodness, faithfulness. —Galatians 5:22-23

Jesus

Believe in your heart that God raised him from the dead, you will be saved.

-Romans 10:9

Come to me, all you who are weary and burdened, and I will give you rest.

-Matthew 11:28

You will keep in perfect peace those whose minds are steadfast, because they trust in you.

-Isaiah 26:3

He gives strength to the weary and increases the power of the weak.

−Isaiah 40:29

If any of you lacks wisdom, you should ask God, who gives generously to all without finding fault, and it will be given to you.

-James 1:5

Their idols are like scarecrows in a cucumber field, and they cannot speak; they have to be carried, for they cannot walk. Do not be afraid of them, for they cannot do evil, neither is it in them to good.

-Jeremiah 10:5

Do not fear, beasts of the field,
For the pastures of the
wilderness have turned green,
For the tree has borne its fruit,
The fig tree and the vine have
yielded in full. NASB

-Joel 2:22

Do not tremble and do not be afraid; Have I not long since announced it to you and declared it? And you are My witnesses. Is there any God besides Me, Or is there any other Rock? I know of none.

-Isaiah 44:8

In the beginning God created the heavens and the earth.

−Genesis 1:1

Thank You

FOR YOUR

Review

Please Share Your Feedback

We wanted to take a moment to express our sincere gratitude
for using our "Faithful Colors" Coloring Book. Your support means a lot to us.
If you had a positive experience with the book, we would be extremely grateful if
you could take a few minutes to leave a review on the platform you purchased it
from. Your feedback and thoughts about the book would be incredibly valuable
for others who are interested in purchasing it and for us as authors. Your review
will help spread the word and reach more people who love coloring.
Thank you again for your support.

Made in the USA
Las Vegas, NV
12 March 2024

87096793R00059